I0466068

ECHO DOT 5TH GEN

GEN

The Insider's Guide

*Hidden Features and Pro Tips to Elevate
Your Smart Home Experience*

Musk James S.

Table of Contents

Introduction

As you hold this book in your hands, you're embarking on a journey into the heart of modern technology, where convenience, innovation, and intelligence converge to transform the way we live. Within these pages, you'll discover the secrets, the hidden gems, and the expert insights that will elevate your smart home experience to new heights.

But why focus on the Echo Dot 5th Generation, you might ask? Well, dear reader, because it's not just a device—it's a gateway to a world of possibilities. It's the voice at your command, the assistant by your side, and the orchestrator of your connected life.

In this guide, we'll delve deep into the realm of the Echo Dot, uncovering its myriad features, unlocking its full potential, and revealing the tips and tricks that will revolutionize the way you interact with your smart home ecosystem.

So why is mastering the Echo Dot essential? Because it's more than just a gadget—it's a conduit for convenience, a facilitator of efficiency, and a catalyst for transformation. Whether you're a tech enthusiast, a smart home aficionado, or a curious beginner, mastering the Echo Dot is the key to unlocking a world of possibilities.

Join me as we embark on this exhilarating journey together, where every page holds the promise of discovery, every word ignites the spark of curiosity, and every insight brings us closer to the pinnacle of smart home innovation. Get ready to unleash the full potential of your Echo Dot 5th Generation and elevate your smart home experience like never before.

Chapter 1:

Getting Started with Echo Dot 5th Gen

Setting up your Echo Dot is the first step towards immersing yourself in the world of smart home convenience. Follow these simple steps for a seamless installation process:

1. **Choose the Perfect Spot**: Select a location for your Echo Dot that has strong Wi-Fi coverage and is centrally located within your home for optimal performance.

2. **Plug It In**: Once you've chosen the ideal spot, plug your Echo Dot into a power outlet using the provided power adapter. Ensure that the device is securely connected and ready to power on.

3. **Download the Alexa App**: To complete the setup process, download the Alexa app from your preferred app store onto your smartphone or

tablet. The app is available for both iOS and Android devices.

4. **Follow the In-App Instructions**: Open the Alexa app and follow the step-by-step instructions provided to set up your Echo Dot. The app will guide you through connecting your device to your Wi-Fi network and registering it to your Amazon account.

5. **Wait for the Setup**: During the setup process, the light ring on your Echo Dot will illuminate orange, indicating that it's in setup mode. Once the setup is complete, the light ring will turn blue, signaling that your Echo Dot is ready for action.

6. **Customize Your Settings**: After the initial setup, take some time to customize your Echo Dot settings according to your preferences. You can adjust various settings such as the device's

wake word, language, and more within the Alexa app.

By following these simple steps, you'll have your Echo Dot up and running in no time, ready to assist you with a wide range of tasks and commands. Get ready to experience the convenience and efficiency of voice-controlled technology at your fingertips.

Understanding the hardware features and functionality

To fully harness the power of your Echo Dot 5th Generation, it's essential to understand its hardware features and functionality. Let's dive into a comprehensive overview:

1. Front-Firing Speaker: The Echo Dot 5th Generation boasts a 1.73-inch front-firing speaker, delivering crisp, clear sound quality for your music, podcasts, audiobooks, and more. Despite its compact size, this speaker produces surprisingly robust audio that can fill a room with rich sound.

2. Microphone Array: Beneath the mesh covering of the Echo Dot are strategically placed microphones that pick up your voice commands from across the room. These far-field microphones utilize advanced beamforming technology to isolate your voice and filter out background noise, ensuring accurate and reliable voice recognition.

3. Top Controls: On the top surface of the Echo Dot, you'll find tactile controls for easy manual operation. These include buttons for muting the microphone, adjusting the volume up and down, and activating the device's action button to summon Alexa manually.

4. Light Ring: Located around the circumference of the Echo Dot's base, the light ring serves as a visual indicator of the device's status. It illuminates in various colors and patterns to convey information such as the device's power status, Wi-Fi connectivity, and notifications.

5. Motion Sensor and Temperature Sensor: Unique to the 5th Generation Echo Dot, this model features built-in motion and temperature sensors. These sensors enable advanced smart home automation capabilities, allowing you to trigger actions based on detected motion or changes in temperature.

6. Tap Gesture: Another convenient feature of the Echo Dot is its tap gesture functionality. By tapping the top surface of the device, you can perform actions such as playing or pausing music, ending a phone call, stopping a timer, or snoozing an alarm.

7. Connectivity Options: The Echo Dot 5th Generation supports both Wi-Fi and Bluetooth connectivity. You can connect it to your home Wi-Fi network for seamless access to online services and smart home integration. Additionally, you can pair it with Bluetooth-enabled devices for audio streaming or use it as a Wi-Fi range extender if you have compatible Amazon-owned Eero Wi-Fi equipment.

Understanding these hardware features and functionalities will enable you to make the most of your Echo Dot 5th Generation. Whether you're enjoying your favorite music, controlling smart home devices, or accessing information with voice commands, this versatile device is your gateway to a smarter, more connected home ecosystem.

Navigating the Alexa App

The Alexa app serves as the central hub for managing and customizing your Echo Dot experience. In this comprehensive guide, we'll explore essential settings and configurations to help you navigate the Alexa app effectively:

1. Device Management: Access the "Devices" tab in the Alexa app to view and manage all your Echo devices. From here, you can rename devices, group them for multi-room audio playback, and control individual device settings.

2. Wi-Fi Setup: Ensure your Echo Dot is connected to your Wi-Fi network for seamless operation. Navigate to the "Devices" tab, select your Echo Dot, and choose "Change" next to the Wi-Fi Network to update its connection settings.

3. Alexa Skills: Explore the "Skills & Games" section to discover and enable new Alexa skills. Skills are voice-driven capabilities that enhance your Echo Dot's functionality, ranging from productivity tools to entertainment apps.

4. Smart Home Integration: Integrate your Echo Dot with compatible smart home devices to control lights, thermostats, and more with voice commands. Visit the "Smart Home" tab to discover and connect devices from popular brands.

5. Routines and Automation: Create custom routines to automate tasks and streamline your daily routines. With routines, you can schedule actions, trigger them with voice commands, or automate them based on specific conditions.

6. Privacy and Security: Review and manage your Echo Dot's privacy and security settings to control data sharing and enhance device security. Customize settings related to voice history, device usage, and third-party app permissions.

7. Communication Features: Explore communication features such as Drop In, Announcements, and Calling to stay connected with friends and family. Enable these features and customize settings to suit your preferences.

8. Voice Responses and Languages: Customize your Echo Dot's voice responses and language preferences to personalize your interaction experience. Choose from a variety of available voices and adjust settings for language, accent, and speech speed.

9. Music and Media Services: Set up your preferred music and media services to enjoy seamless playback on your Echo Dot. Connect services like Amazon Music, Spotify, or Apple Music to access your favorite songs, playlists, and podcasts.

10. Alexa App Settings: Explore additional settings within the Alexa app to fine-tune your Echo Dot experience. Adjust settings related to notifications, reminders, alarms, and more to customize your device according to your preferences.

By familiarizing yourself with these essential settings and configurations in the Alexa app, you'll be able to tailor your Echo Dot experience to meet your unique needs and preferences. Whether you're enhancing your smart home setup, discovering new skills, or optimizing device settings, the Alexa app is your go-to tool for unlocking the full potential of your Echo Dot.

Chapter 2:

Exploring the Echo Dot Hardware

Let's take a closer look at the physical components of the Echo Dot 5th Generation to understand its design and functionality:

1. Compact Design: The Echo Dot 5th Gen maintains its iconic compact form factor, making it suitable for any space in your home. With dimensions of approximately 3.9 inches in diameter and 3.5 inches in height, it blends seamlessly into its surroundings while delivering powerful performance.

2. Mesh Fabric Finish: The Echo Dot features a sleek mesh fabric finish that adds a touch of elegance to its design. The fabric covering not only enhances its aesthetic appeal but also allows sound to pass through easily, ensuring optimal audio quality.

3. Front-Facing Speaker: Positioned at the top of the device, the front-facing speaker delivers crisp, clear sound with enhanced bass response. Whether you're listening to music, podcasts, or audiobooks, the Echo Dot offers an immersive audio experience that fills the room.

4. Control Buttons: On the top surface of the Echo Dot, you'll find control buttons for easy access to essential functions. These include a mute button to disable the microphones, volume up and down buttons for adjusting the audio level, and an action button for activating Alexa.

5. LED Light Ring: Encircling the bottom edge of the Echo Dot is an LED light ring that serves as a visual indicator of the device's status. The light ring illuminates in various colors to convey different information, such as orange during setup, blue when Alexa is activated, red when the microphone is muted, and yellow for notifications.

6. Microphone Array: Beneath the mesh fabric covering, the Echo Dot houses a microphone array that enables far-field voice recognition. With multiple microphones strategically positioned around the device, the Echo Dot can pick up voice commands from across the room, even in noisy environments.

7. Power Port: Located at the back of the device is the power port, where you connect the included power adapter to provide electricity to the Echo Dot. Ensure the device is plugged into a power source for continuous operation and functionality.

8. Motion and Temperature Sensors: Unique to the 5th Generation Echo Dot, built-in motion and temperature sensors add additional functionality to the device. These sensors can detect motion in the surrounding area and measure ambient temperature, enabling advanced features such as motion-triggered routines and temperature-based automations.

By understanding the physical components of the Echo Dot 5th Generation, you can fully appreciate its design and capabilities. Whether you're setting up the device, adjusting settings, or simply enjoying its audio performance, each component plays a vital role in delivering a seamless and immersive smart home experience.

The significance of the front-firing speaker and top buttons

The front-firing speaker and top buttons of the Echo Dot 5th Generation are integral components that contribute to its functionality and user experience. Let's delve into their significance:

1. Front-Firing Speaker:

- Enhanced Audio Quality: Unlike previous generations, the Echo Dot 5th Gen features a front-firing speaker that delivers improved audio quality. By positioning the speaker at the front of the device, sound is projected directly towards the listener, resulting in clearer vocals and enhanced bass response.

- Immersive Sound Experience: Whether you're streaming music, listening to podcasts, or engaging in hands-free calls, the front-firing speaker ensures an immersive sound experience that fills the room. Enjoy rich, full-bodied sound that surpasses expectations for a device of its size.

- Balanced Acoustic Performance: The design of the front-firing speaker is optimized to deliver balanced acoustic performance across a wide range of frequencies. From crisp highs to deep lows, the Echo Dot offers consistent audio quality that adapts to different types of content.

2. Top Buttons:

- Mute Button: The top surface of the Echo Dot features a dedicated mute button that allows you to temporarily disable the device's microphones. Pressing the mute button ensures privacy by preventing Alexa from listening for wake words or commands. When muted, the LED light ring turns red to indicate that the microphones are inactive.

- Volume Controls: Conveniently located on the top of the device are volume up and down buttons, which allow you to adjust the audio level to your preference. Whether you want to increase the volume for music playback or decrease it for a quieter environment, the tactile buttons provide tactile feedback for effortless control.

- Action Button: Positioned alongside the volume controls is the action button, which serves multiple functions. Pressing the action button activates Alexa, allowing you to issue voice commands or interact with the device. You can ask questions, play music, set reminders, control smart home devices, and more, all with a simple press of a button.

By understanding the significance of the front-firing speaker and top buttons, you can make the most of your Echo Dot 5th Generation experience. Whether you're enjoying high-quality audio or effortlessly controlling the device's functions, these components play a crucial role in delivering a seamless and intuitive user experience.

Leveraging the built-in motion sensor and temperature sensor for smart home automation

The Echo Dot 5th Generation comes equipped with built-in motion and temperature sensors, unlocking a world of possibilities for smart home automation. Let's explore how you can leverage these sensors to enhance your living space:

1. Motion Sensor:

- Automated Lighting: With the motion sensor, you can automate your lighting based on movement within a room. For example, configure smart bulbs to turn on automatically when motion is detected and turn off after a specified period of inactivity. This not only enhances convenience but also contributes to energy efficiency by eliminating the need for manual control.

- Security Enhancements: The motion sensor can also serve as a security feature by triggering alerts or activating surveillance cameras in response to detected motion. Receive notifications on your smartphone when motion is detected, allowing you to monitor activity in your home remotely and take appropriate action if necessary.

- Personalized Experiences: Customize your smart home experience by creating tailored automation routines based on motion events. Whether you want lights to dim when you enter a room or music to play when you walk by, the possibilities are endless with the Echo Dot's motion sensor capabilities.

2. Temperature Sensor:

- Climate Control: Monitor and manage the temperature in your home with the Echo Dot's built-in temperature sensor. Integrate the device with compatible smart thermostats to adjust heating and cooling settings based on ambient temperature conditions. Create schedules, set temperature thresholds, and optimize energy usage for increased comfort and cost savings.

- Weather Alerts: Stay informed about weather conditions both indoors and outdoors using the temperature sensor. Access real-time temperature data through the Alexa app and receive weather alerts or updates tailored to your location. Plan your day accordingly and make informed decisions based on current temperature readings.

- Temperature-Based Triggers: Use temperature readings as triggers for smart home automation routines. For example, set up a routine to adjust blinds or curtains automatically based on changes in temperature throughout the day. Create a comfortable environment that adapts to your preferences without manual intervention.

By leveraging the built-in motion and temperature sensors of the Echo Dot 5th Generation, you can create a smarter, more responsive home environment. From enhancing security to optimizing energy efficiency, these sensors empower you to automate tasks and customize your living space according to your needs and preferences.

Chapter 3:

Audio Features and Music Streaming

The Echo Dot 5th Generation isn't just a smart assistant — it's also a powerful speaker that can elevate your audio experience. Let's delve into how you can unlock the full potential of the Echo Dot as a high-quality speaker:

1. Improved Sound Quality:

- Despite its compact size, the Echo Dot delivers impressive sound quality with its upgraded speaker design. Featuring a 1.6-inch front-firing speaker, the device produces clear highs, rich mids, and deep bass for a well-balanced audio experience. Whether you're streaming music, listening to podcasts, or enjoying audiobooks, the Echo Dot delivers crisp, immersive sound that fills the room.

2. Music Streaming Options:

- With the Echo Dot, you have access to a wide range of music streaming services, including Amazon Music, Spotify, Apple Music, and more. Simply link your preferred music service to your Alexa account through the Alexa app, and you can request songs, albums, playlists, and radio stations with just your voice. Explore new artists, rediscover old favorites, and enjoy personalized music recommendations tailored to your tastes.

3. Voice-Controlled Playback:

- Take hands-free control of your music playback using voice commands with Alexa. Whether you want to play, pause, skip tracks, or adjust the volume, simply say the wake word followed by your command, and the Echo Dot will respond instantly. Enjoy the convenience of controlling your music without having to reach for your phone or manually interact with the device.

4. Speaker Grouping:

- Create speaker groups with multiple Echo devices to synchronize music playback throughout your home. Whether you're hosting a party or simply moving from room to room, speaker groups allow you to enjoy seamless audio streaming in every corner of your house. Set up custom groups using the Alexa app and effortlessly switch between individual devices or synchronized groups as needed.

5. Bluetooth Connectivity:

- Expand your audio options by connecting the Echo Dot to external Bluetooth speakers or headphones. Whether you prefer the convenience of wireless headphones or the immersive sound of a premium speaker system, Bluetooth connectivity allows you to customize your listening experience to suit your preferences. Simply pair your Bluetooth device with the Echo Dot, and you're ready to enjoy your favorite content with enhanced audio quality.

Unlocking the power of the Echo Dot as a high-quality speaker opens up a world of possibilities for immersive audio entertainment. Whether you're enjoying music, podcasts, audiobooks, or more, the Echo Dot delivers exceptional sound performance that enhances your listening experience and transforms your home into a hub of entertainment.

The music streaming options: Spotify, Amazon Music, and more

When it comes to streaming music on your Echo Dot 5th Generation, you have a plethora of options to choose from. Let's explore some of the most popular music streaming services available:

1. Amazon Music: As an Amazon device, the Echo Dot seamlessly integrates with Amazon Music, offering access to millions of songs, albums, playlists, and stations. With Amazon Music, you can enjoy ad-free streaming, personalized recommendations, and exclusive content, including Amazon Originals. Whether you're in the mood for chart-topping hits, classic favorites, or niche genres, Amazon Music has something for every musical taste.

2. Spotify: Spotify is one of the world's leading music streaming platforms, known for its vast catalog of songs, curated playlists, and personalized recommendations. With Spotify Premium, you can enjoy on-demand access to millions of tracks without ads, along with features like offline listening and unlimited skips. Simply link your Spotify account to your Echo Dot and use voice commands to play your favorite artists, albums, playlists, and podcasts.

3. Apple Music: If you're an Apple user, you can access your Apple Music library directly on your Echo Dot. With Apple Music, you can stream millions of songs, listen to curated playlists, and explore exclusive content from your favorite artists. Whether you're an iPhone, iPad, Mac, or Apple Watch user, Apple Music seamlessly syncs across all your devices, allowing you to enjoy your music wherever you go.

4. Pandora: Pandora offers personalized radio stations based on your musical preferences, making it easy to discover new artists and genres. With Pandora, you can create custom stations, thumbs up or thumbs down songs to refine your recommendations, and access curated playlists curated by music experts. Simply link your Pandora account to your Echo Dot and enjoy endless hours of personalized music streaming.

5. Tidal: Tidal is known for its high-fidelity audio quality and extensive catalog of exclusive content, including high-resolution music and music videos. With Tidal HiFi, you can stream lossless audio in CD quality, providing an immersive listening experience that's unmatched by standard streaming services. Whether you're an audiophile or simply appreciate crystal-clear sound, Tidal offers premium audio streaming that takes your music enjoyment to the next level.

6. Deezer: Deezer offers a diverse selection of music, podcasts, and radio stations, catering to a wide range of musical tastes and preferences. With Deezer, you can explore curated playlists, discover new artists, and enjoy personalized recommendations based on your listening history. Whether you're into pop, rock, hip-hop, jazz, or classical music, Deezer has something for everyone. With a multitude of music streaming options available on the Echo Dot 5th Generation, you can tailor your listening experience to suit your individual preferences and discover new music from around the world. Whether you're a fan of mainstream hits, underground indie bands, or niche genres, there's a streaming service that's perfect for you. Simply link your preferred music service to your Echo Dot and start enjoying a world of music at your fingertips.

Creating speaker groups for multi-room music playback

With the Echo Dot 5th Generation, you have the flexibility to create speaker groups, allowing you to enjoy synchronized multi-room music playback throughout your home. Here's how you can create speaker groups for a seamless audio experience:

1. **Open the Alexa App:**
   - Launch the Alexa app on your smartphone or tablet. Ensure that your Echo Dot devices are connected to the same Wi-Fi network as your mobile device.

2. **Navigate to Devices:**
   - Tap on the "Devices" icon located in the bottom right corner of the app. This will take you to a list of all your Alexa-compatible devices.

3. **Select Speaker Groups:**

   • Scroll down and tap on "Speaker Groups." Here, you'll find the option to create and manage speaker groups for multi-room audio playback.

4. **Create a New Speaker Group:**

   • To create a new speaker group, tap on the "+" icon or the "Create Group" button. You'll be prompted to select the devices you want to include in the group.

5. **Choose Echo Dot Devices:**

   • Select the Echo Dot devices you want to add to the speaker group. You can choose multiple Echo Dots located in different rooms to create a multi-room audio setup.

6. **Name Your Speaker Group:**

   • After selecting the devices, give your speaker group a descriptive name that reflects its location or purpose. For example, you could name it "Living Room," "Kitchen," or "Whole House."

7. **Save Your Settings:**

   - Once you've named your speaker group and selected the desired devices, tap on the "Save" or "Create" button to finalize your settings. Your new speaker group will now appear in the list of available speaker groups.

8. **Enjoy Multi-Room Music Playback:**

   - With your speaker group set up, you can now enjoy synchronized music playback across all the Echo Dot devices included in the group. Simply ask Alexa to play your favorite songs, albums, or playlists, and they'll be streamed simultaneously on all the devices in the selected group.

By creating speaker groups, you can enhance your listening experience and fill your home with music from every corner. Whether you're hosting a party, cooking in the kitchen, or relaxing in the living room, multi-room music playback ensures that your favorite tunes are always within earshot.

Chapter 4:

Communication and Smart Home Controls

The Echo Dot 5th Generation isn't just a smart speaker—it's a powerful communication hub that allows you to stay connected with friends and family in new and innovative ways. Here's how you can harness its communication features to make announcements, drop in on other Echo devices, and make phone calls:

1. **Making Announcements:**
   - With the Echo Dot, you can broadcast announcements to all Echo devices within your home. Whether you need to alert your family members about dinner time or remind them of an upcoming event, making announcements is quick and easy.
   - Simply say, "Alexa, announce [your message]," and Alexa will broadcast your

message to all connected Echo devices. Your announcement will be heard loud and clear throughout your home, ensuring that everyone stays informed and up-to-date.

2. **Dropping In on Other Echo Devices:**
   - Drop In is a feature that allows you to instantly connect with other Echo devices in your household, providing a convenient way to check in on family members or have a quick conversation without picking up the phone.
   - To drop in on another Echo device, simply say, "Alexa, drop in on [device name]." You'll be instantly connected to the chosen device, and you can start speaking without the need for them to answer.
   - It's important to note that Drop In is an opt-in feature, meaning both the sender and receiver must enable Drop In permissions in their Alexa app settings for it to work.

3. **Making Phone Calls:**
    - With the Echo Dot, you can make hands-free phone calls to anyone in your contacts list or to specific phone numbers. Whether you need to catch up with a friend or check in with a family member, making phone calls with Alexa is convenient and efficient.
    - Simply say, "Alexa, call [contact name]" or "Alexa, call [phone number]," and Alexa will initiate the call using your Echo Dot. You can also answer incoming calls by saying, "Alexa, answer."
    - To set up calling on your Echo Dot, make sure your contacts are synced with the Alexa app and that you've enabled calling permissions in the app settings.

By harnessing these communication features, you can stay connected with your loved ones and streamline your daily communication tasks with ease. Whether you're making announcements, dropping in on other Echo devices, or making phone calls, the Echo Dot provides a convenient and hands-free way to stay in touch with the people who matter most.

<u>Integrating Echo Dot with smart home devices</u>

Integrating your Echo Dot with smart home devices opens up a world of possibilities for automating tasks and controlling your home with just your voice. Here's how you can set up routines, automations, and voice commands to seamlessly integrate your Echo Dot with your smart home devices:

1. **Setting Up Routines:**
    *   Routines allow you to automate multiple actions with a single voice command or schedule. With the Alexa app, you can create custom routines tailored to your specific needs and preferences.
    *   Begin by opening the Alexa app and navigating to the Routines section. From

there, tap on "Create Routine" and choose a trigger phrase that will activate your routine.

- Next, select the actions you want your routine to perform. This could include turning on lights, adjusting thermostats, playing music, or even delivering a custom announcement.

- Once you've configured your routine, save it, and give it a try by saying your trigger phrase to your Echo Dot. Your smart home devices will spring into action, making your routine a seamless part of your daily life.

2. **Automating Tasks with Smart Home Devices:**

- Smart home devices like smart lights, thermostats, and plugs can be integrated with your Echo Dot to automate tasks and simplify your daily routine.

- Use the Alexa app to set up automations that trigger based on specific conditions or events. For example, you could set your lights to turn on automatically when motion is detected or adjust your thermostat based on your location.

- By automating tasks with your smart home devices, you can save time and energy while enjoying the convenience of a fully connected home.

3. **Voice Commands for Smart Home Control:**

- Your Echo Dot allows you to control your smart home devices using simple voice commands. Whether you want to turn on lights, adjust the temperature, or lock the door, Alexa can handle it all.
- To control your smart home devices with voice commands, simply say, "Alexa, [action] [device name]." For example, "Alexa, turn on the living room lights" or "Alexa, set the thermostat to 72 degrees."

- You can also create groups of smart home devices to control multiple devices with a single command. For instance, you could create a group called "Downstairs" that includes all the lights and plugs in your downstairs area.

By setting up routines, automations, and voice commands, you can seamlessly integrate your Echo Dot with your smart home devices and enjoy the convenience of hands-free control over your home environment. Whether you're automating tasks, controlling devices with voice commands, or creating custom routines, the Echo Dot offers endless possibilities for enhancing your smart home experience.

Maximizing the Alexa Guard feature for enhanced home security

The Alexa Guard feature provides an additional layer of security for your home by leveraging your

Echo Dot's capabilities. Here's how you can maximize the Alexa Guard feature to enhance your home security:

1. **Setting Up Alexa Guard:**
   - Begin by opening the Alexa app on your smartphone and navigating to the Guard section.
   - Follow the prompts to enable Alexa Guard and select your preferences for Away Lighting, Smart Alerts, and Emergency Helpline.

2. **Away Lighting:**
   - When you set your Alexa Guard to Away mode, it can simulate occupancy by turning your smart lights on and off at random intervals. This creates the illusion that someone is home, deterring potential intruders.
   - To activate Away Lighting, simply say, "Alexa, I'm leaving," or set it manually in the Alexa app before you leave home.

3. **Smart Alerts:**
   - Alexa Guard can listen for specific sounds, such as smoke alarms, carbon monoxide detectors, or glass breaking. If it detects any of these sounds while you're away, it will send you a notification on your smartphone.
   - Ensure that your Echo Dot is placed in a central location where it can effectively listen for these sounds and alert you in case of an emergency.

4. **Emergency Helpline (Alexa Guard Plus):**
   - If you subscribe to Alexa Guard Plus, you gain access to additional features like emergency helpline support. In case of an emergency, you can use voice commands to connect directly with trained agents who can dispatch help to your location.

- To activate emergency helpline support, simply say, "Alexa, call for help," or configure it in the Alexa app settings.

5. **Testing Alexa Guard:**
   - It's essential to test Alexa Guard regularly to ensure that it's functioning correctly. You can do this by activating Away mode and triggering various sounds, such as breaking glass or smoke alarms, to see if you receive notifications on your smartphone.
   - Regular testing helps ensure that Alexa Guard is ready to protect your home when you need it most.

By maximizing the Alexa Guard feature, you can enhance the security of your home and gain peace of mind knowing that your Echo Dot is actively monitoring for potential threats. Whether you're using Away Lighting to simulate occupancy, receiving Smart Alerts for detected sounds, or accessing emergency helpline support with Alexa

Guard Plus, your Echo Dot is a valuable tool for keeping your home safe and secure.

Chapter 5:

Advanced Tips and Tricks

The Echo Dot 5th Generation may seem like a simple smart speaker at first glance, but beneath its sleek exterior lies a world of hidden features and functionalities waiting to be discovered. In this section, we'll delve into some of these lesser-known capabilities that can elevate your experience with the device.

1. **Voice Profiles:** Did you know that you can set up voice profiles for different members of your household? By doing so, Alexa can personalize responses based on who is speaking, providing tailored music recommendations, calendar updates, and more.

2. **Follow-Up Mode:** Enable Follow-Up Mode to allow Alexa to listen for additional requests after the initial command without having to repeat the wake word. This seamless interaction makes it

easier to carry out multiple tasks in quick succession.

3. **Brief Mode:** Tired of hearing Alexa's verbose responses? Turn on Brief Mode to receive shorter, more concise confirmations for commands like turning off lights or setting timers. It's a great way to streamline interactions with your Echo Dot.

4. **Whisper Mode:** Need to ask Alexa a question without waking up the entire household? Whisper Mode allows you to speak softly to your Echo Dot, and Alexa will respond in a whisper as well, maintaining the tranquility of your home environment.

5. **Drop-In with Alexa-enabled Devices:** If you have multiple Echo devices in your home, you can use Drop-In to establish instant two-way communication between them. Whether you're checking in on a family member in another room

or announcing dinner time, Drop-In makes communication effortless.

6. **Amazon Sidewalk Integration:** Take advantage of Amazon Sidewalk, a shared network that extends the range of your Echo Dot and other compatible devices beyond the confines of your home Wi-Fi network. This feature can be particularly useful for outdoor smart home devices like security cameras and lights.

7. **Voice Calling and Messaging:** Use your Echo Dot to make hands-free voice calls to friends and family who also have Echo devices or the Alexa app. You can also send voice messages, making it easy to stay connected with loved ones, even when your hands are full.

8. **Voice Purchasing with Voice Code:** Worried about unauthorized purchases? Set up a voice code to confirm any orders made through your

Echo Dot. This adds an extra layer of security and peace of mind when shopping with Alexa.

By exploring these hidden features and functionalities, you'll unlock the full potential of your Echo Dot 5th Generation and enhance your smart home experience in ways you never thought possible. So go ahead, dive in, and discover what else your Echo Dot can do!

Optimizing voice commands for efficiency and convenience

One of the most powerful features of the Echo Dot 5th Generation is its ability to respond to voice commands, providing a hands-free and seamless way to interact with your smart home devices. In this section, we'll explore how you can optimize your voice commands for maximum efficiency and convenience.

1. **Clear and Concise Commands:** When issuing voice commands to your Echo Dot, it's essential to be clear and concise. Avoid using ambiguous phrases and instead opt for straightforward commands that Alexa can easily understand. For example, instead of saying, "Can you please turn off the lights in the living room?" simply say, "Turn off the living room lights."

2. **Use Keywords:** Alexa responds best to specific keywords or trigger words that indicate a command is being given. Some common keywords include "Alexa," "Echo," or "Computer," depending on your wake word settings. Begin your command with one of these keywords to ensure Alexa recognizes that you're addressing her.

3. **Group Commands:** Take advantage of Alexa's ability to understand grouped commands. Instead of issuing commands one by one, you can string multiple actions together in a single

sentence. For example, you could say, "Alexa, turn off the lights in the living room and set the thermostat to 72 degrees."

4. **Utilize Routines:** Routines allow you to automate multiple tasks with a single command. Create custom routines in the Alexa app to trigger a series of actions based on specific triggers or times of day. For example, you could set up a "Goodnight" routine that turns off lights, locks doors, and adjusts the thermostat when you say, "Alexa, goodnight."

5. **Customize Commands:** Alexa offers a range of customization options for voice commands. In the Alexa app, you can create custom voice commands for specific actions, devices, or skills. This allows you to tailor your interactions with Alexa to suit your preferences and needs.

6. **Practice Natural Language:** Alexa is designed to understand natural language

commands, so feel free to phrase your requests in a way that feels comfortable to you. Whether you're asking for the weather forecast, setting reminders, or playing music, Alexa can interpret a wide range of conversational prompts.

7. **Provide Feedback:** If Alexa misunderstands a command or fails to execute it correctly, provide feedback to help improve her responsiveness over time. You can do this by using the voice feedback feature or submitting feedback through the Alexa app.

By optimizing your voice commands for efficiency and convenience, you can make the most of your Echo Dot and enjoy a more seamless smart home experience. Whether you're controlling lights, playing music, or managing your calendar, Alexa is ready to assist you with just a simple voice command. So go ahead, speak up, and let Alexa do the rest!

Chapter 6:

Troubleshooting and FAQs

While the Echo Dot 5th Generation is designed to offer seamless performance, occasional connectivity and functionality issues may arise. In this section, we'll address some common issues and provide troubleshooting tips to help you resolve them quickly and effectively.

1. **Wi-Fi Connectivity Problems:** If your Echo Dot is having trouble connecting to your Wi-Fi network, try the following steps:

   - Ensure that your Echo Dot is within range of your Wi-Fi router and that there are no obstructions blocking the signal.
   - Restart your Wi-Fi router and Echo Dot by unplugging them for a few seconds and then plugging them back in.

- Check for any software updates for your Echo Dot and install them if available.
- Try connecting your Echo Dot to a different Wi-Fi network to see if the issue persists.

2. **Bluetooth Pairing Issues:** If you're experiencing problems with Bluetooth connectivity, try these troubleshooting steps:
   - Make sure that your Echo Dot and the Bluetooth device you're trying to pair are in pairing mode and within range of each other.
   - Check that the Bluetooth device is compatible with the Echo Dot and that it's not already connected to another device.
   - Forget the Bluetooth device from your Echo Dot's settings in the Alexa app and then try pairing it again from scratch.
   - Restart both your Echo Dot and the Bluetooth device to reset their connection.

3. **Unresponsive Voice Commands:** If Alexa is not responding to your voice commands, consider the following solutions:

   - Check that the microphone on your Echo Dot is not muted. You can unmute it by pressing the microphone button on the top of the device.

   - Ensure that your Echo Dot is connected to the internet and that there are no network issues affecting its performance.

   - Try rephrasing your voice commands or speaking more clearly to improve Alexa's understanding.

   - If Alexa is still unresponsive, restart your Echo Dot by unplugging it for a few seconds and then plugging it back in.

4. **Software Glitches and Errors:** If you encounter software glitches or errors on your Echo Dot, try the following troubleshooting steps:

- Restart your Echo Dot by unplugging it for a few seconds and then plugging it back in.
- Check for any software updates for your Echo Dot in the Alexa app and install them if available.
- Reset your Echo Dot to its factory settings as a last resort. Note that this will erase all settings and preferences, so use this option with caution.

5. **Contacting Customer Support:** If you've tried the above troubleshooting steps and are still experiencing issues with your Echo Dot, consider contacting Amazon customer support for further assistance. They can provide personalized troubleshooting advice and may be able to offer a solution or replacement if necessary.

By following these troubleshooting tips, you can resolve common connectivity and functionality issues with your Echo Dot 5th Generation and enjoy a seamless smart home experience.

Conclusion

Congratulations on completing the Insider's Guide to the Echo Dot 5th Generation! Throughout this book, we've covered a wide range of topics and provided you with valuable insights and tips to help you make the most of your Echo Dot device.

In summary, we've explored everything from setting up your Echo Dot and understanding its hardware features to leveraging its communication capabilities and integrating it with other smart home devices. We've delved into the world of music streaming, voice commands, and hidden features, empowering you to unlock the full potential of your Echo Dot.

As you continue to explore and experiment with your Echo Dot, remember that the possibilities are endless. Whether you're using it to play music, control your smart home devices, or simply make your life more convenient, there's always something new to discover and try.

In conclusion, I encourage you to stay curious and proactive in your journey with smart home technology. By staying informed and empowered, you can take full advantage of the capabilities of your Echo Dot and enhance your everyday life in ways you never imagined.

Thank you for joining us on this journey, and here's to many more exciting adventures with your Echo Dot 5th Generation!

www.ingramcontent.com/pod-product-compliance
Lightning Source LLC
Chambersburg PA
CBHW070130230526
45472CB00004B/1497